Contents

Grilled Sardines & Arugula 3
Salmon Panzanella 3
Seafood Couscous Paella 4
Greek Salmon Burgers 4
Tuna Pasta with Artichokes 5
Chicken & Garbanzo Salad 6
Mediterranean Tuna Salad 6
Vegetable Omelet 7
Salted Breakfast Potatoes 8
Huevos Revuletos 8
Banana Nut Oatmeal 9
Easy Mediterranean Eggs 9
Mediterranean Omelet 10
Flank Steak & Spinach Salad 10
Easy Chicken Greek Salad 11
Cheese Stuffed Tomatoes 11
Tomato & Pasta Bowl 12
Garlic Broiled Sardines 13
Fruity Chicken Salad 13
Mustard Trout with Apples 14
Chicken Milano 15
Sicilian Lemon Chicken 15
Braised Chicken & Olives 16
Lamb & Couscous Salad 17
Mediterranean Salmon 18
Seafood Linguine 19
Ginger Shrimp & Tomato Relish 20
Shrimp & Pasta 20
Poached Cod 21
Mussels in White Wine 22
Dilly Salmon 22

Chicken & Vegetable Soup	23
Sautéed Spinach & Pine Nuts	23
French Onion Soup	24
Braised Kale & Tomatoes	25
Anchovy & Olive Salad	25
Greek Potatoes	26
Spicy Eggplant	26
Spiced Turkey & Grapefruit Relish	27
Greek Chicken Penne	28
Lemon Caper Chicken	28
Gnocchi with Shrimp	29
Mediterranean Fried Rice	30
Swiss Chard & Olives	30
Cucumber & Pesto Boats	31
Citrus Melon	31
Yogurt Mousse & Sour Cherry Topping	32
Caramel Roasted Figs	32
Pomegranate Poached Pears	33
Marinated Berries	33

LUNCH RECIPES

GRILLED SARDINES & ARUGULA

Serves: 2

Time: 15 Minutes

Ingredients:

- 1 Bunch Baby Arugula, Trimmed
- 1 Teaspoon Olive Oil
- 8 Ounces Sardines, Fresh, Innards & Gills Removed
- Sea Salt & Black Pepper to Taste
- Lemon Wedges to Garnish

Directions:

1. Start by preparing your grill and then rinsing the arugula. Shake off any excess water, and then place it on a platter. Put the arugula to the side.
2. Rinse the sardines using cold water, and rub them to remove the scales. Wipe them dry, and then get out a bowl. Combine your olive oil and sardine. Toss so that your sardines are well coated.
3. Grill your sardines using high heat for three minutes per side, and then season with salt and pepper. Transfer to plates lined in arugula, and then add your lemon wedges to garnish.

SALMON PANZANELLA

Serves: 2

Time: 10 Minutes

Ingredients:

- 1/2 lb. Center Cut Salmon, Skinned & Sliced into 2 Portions
- 4 Kalamata Olives, Chopped & Pitted
- 1 1/2 Tablespoons Olive Oil
- 1/2 Tablespoon Capers, Chopped
- 1 Tomato, Cut into 1 Inch Pieces
- 1 Slice Stale Bread, Whole Grain, Chopped into 1 Inch Cubes
- 1 1/2 Tablespoons Red Wine Vinegar
- 1 Small Cucumber, Cut into 1 Inch Cubes
- 3 Tablespoons Basil, Fresh & Chopped Fine
- 3 Tablespoons Red Onion, Sliced Thin

Directions:

1. Start by setting your grill to high and then get out a bowl. Whisk your capers, olives, vinegar and pepper until it's well combined, and then add in your onion, cucumber, bread, tomatoes and basil.
2. Oil the grill rack, and then season your salmon with salt and pepper on both sides. Grill the salmon until it's fully cooked, which will take four to five minutes per side.
3. Divide your salad among four plates, topping with salmon.

SEAFOOD COUSCOUS PAELLA

Serves: 2

Time: 15 Minutes

Ingredients:

- 1/2 Cup Couscous, Whole Wheat
- 4 Ounces Baby Scallops, Tough Muscle Removed
- 4 Ounces Shrimp, Peeled & Deveined
- 2 Teaspoons Olive Oil
- 1 Clove Garlic, Minced
- 1 Onion, Chopped
- 1/2 Teaspoon Fennel Seeds
- 1/2 Teaspoon Thyme
- 1/4 Cup Vegetable Broth
- Sea Salt & Black Pepper to Taste
- 1 Cup Tomatoes, Canned, Diced & No Salt Added with Juice
- Pinch Saffron Threads, Crumbled

Directions:

1. Start by getting out a saucepan, and heat your oil over medium heat. Add in your onion, and cook for three minutes. Make sure to stir regularly to keep it from burning. Add in your garlic, pepper, thyme, salt, saffron and fennel seeds. Cook for about a half a minute more.
2. Stir in the tomatoes and broth, and then bring it all to a simmer. Cover, reducing the heat and simmering for two minutes more.
3. Increase the heat to medium, and then stir in the scallops, cooking for an additional two minutes. Stir occasionally to keep it from sticking.
4. Add the shrimp, cooking for two minutes more.
5. Stir in your couscous, and then cover and remove your pan from heat. Allow it to stand for five minutes before fluffing to serve warm.

GREEK SALMON BURGERS

Serves: 2

Time: 20 Minutes

Ingredients:

- 2 Ciabatta Rolls, Toasted
- 1/8 Cup Feta Cheese, Crumbled
- Sea Salt & Black Pepper to Taste
- 1/4 Cup Cucumber Slices
- 1/4 Cup Panko
- 1 Small Egg Whites
- 1/2 lb. Salmon Fillets, Skinless & Chopped into 2 Inch Pieces

Directions:

1. Get out a food processor pulsing the egg white, panko and salmon together until the salmon is chopped fine.
2. Form into two patties, and then season with salt and pepper.
3. Heat the grill to medium-high, and then grease the grill. Cook the patties for five to seven minutes per side and toast the ciabatta rolls.
4. Top with cucumber slices before serving warm.

TUNA PASTA WITH ARTICHOKES

Serves: 2

Time: 25 Minutes

Ingredients:

- 4 Ounces Tuna Steak, Sliced into 2 Pieces
- 1 Teaspoon Lemon Zest, Fresh
- 2 Tablespoons Olive Oil
- Sea Salt & Black Pepper to Taste
- 1 Teaspoon Rosemary, Fresh & Chopped
- 1/8 Cup Green Olives, Chopped
- 5 Ounces Artichoke Hearts, Frozen & Thawed
- 3 Ounces Penne Pasta, Whole Wheat
- 1 Cup Grape Tomatoes
- 2 Cloves Garlic, Minced
- 1 Tablespoon Lemon Juice, Fresh
- 1/4 Cup White Wine
- 1/8 Cup Basil, Fresh & Chopped

Directions:

1. Start by heating your grill to medium-high heat, and then get out a large pot of water. Bring your water to a boil.

2. Get out a bowl and toss the tuna pieces in with lemon zest, half your rosemary, half your oil, a dash of salt and pepper. And then grill for three minutes per side before putting it on a plate. Cut it to bite sized pieces when the tuna is cool enough to handle.
3. Cook your pasta in the boiling water according to package instructions and then drain when finished.
4. Heat the remaining oil in a skillet using medium heat, adding in your artichoke hearts, remaining rosemary, olives and garlic. Cook for four minutes more, and stir often to keep from burning. Add your wine and tomatoes, and then bring it to a boil for three minutes more. Your wine should have reduced some and your tomatoes should be broken down. Stir in your pasta, lemon juice and tuna pieces. Add another dash of salt, and cook for two minutes. Garnish with a ¼ cup of basil.

CHICKEN & GARBANZO SALAD

Serves: 2
Time: 15 Minutes

Ingredients:

- 4.5 Ounces Chicken Breast, Cooked & Chopped
- 7 Ounces chickpeas
- 1/2 Cup Cucumber, Seeded & Chopped
- 1/8 Cup Mint, Fresh & Chopped
- 1/8 Cup Green Onions, Chopped
- 1/4 Cup Plain Yogurt, Fat Free
- 2 Cloves Garlic, Minced
- 1 Cups Baby Spinach
- 1/6 Cup Feta Cheese, Crumbled
- Sea Salt & Black Pepper to Taste
- 2 Lemon Wedges

Directions:

1. Start by combining all of your ingredients except for your feta, spinach and lemon wedges. Fold in the feat and spinach leaves next.
2. Add in your lemon wedges, and then serve.

MEDITERRANEAN TUNA SALAD

Serves: 2

Time: 15 Minutes

Ingredients:

- 1/4 Cup Lemon Juice, Fresh

- 1/4 Cup Parsley, Fresh & Chopped
- 2 Teaspoons Capers
- 1/2 Red Bell Pepper, Diced Fine
- 1/4 Cup Red Onion, Chopped
- 1 Can Light Tuna, Water Packed & 6 Ounces Each
- 10 Ounces Chickpeas, Canned
- 3/4 Teaspoon Rosemary, Fresh & Chopped Fine
- 2 Tablespoons Olive Oil
- 4 Cups Mixed Salad Greens
- Sea Salt & Black Pepper to Taste

Directions:

1. Combine your tuna, onion, capers, pepper, beans, parsley, rosemary, a tablespoon of oil and your 1/8 cup lemon juice. Season with a dash of salt and pepper, and mix well.
2. Mix your remaining lemon juice, salt and oil in a bowl, adding your salad greens, and toss to coat before serving.

VEGETABLE OMELET

Serves: 2

Time: 30 Minutes

Ingredients:

- 1/2 Teaspoon Olive Oil
- 1 Cup Fennel Bulbs, Fresh & Sliced Thin
- 1/8 Cup Canned Artichoke Hearts, Rinsed, Drained & Chopped
- 1/8 Cup Green Olives, Pitted & Chopped
- 1 Small Roma Tomato, Chopped
- 3 Eggs
- 1/4 Cup Goat Cheese, Crumbled
- Sea Salt & Black Pepper to Taste

Directions:

1. Start by heating the oven to 325, and then get out an ovenproof skillet. Heat your oil over medium-high heat, and cook your fennel bulb for five minutes.
2. Add in your olives, artichoke hearts, and tomato before cooking for an additional three minutes.
3. Get out a bowl and whisk your eggs, salt and pepper together.
4. Pour this egg mixture over the vegetable mixture, and stir to combine.
5. Cook for two minutes, and then sprinkle evenly with goat cheese.
6. Transfer the skillet to the oven, and bake for five minutes. Your eggs should be completely set.
7. Remove from the skillet, and allow it to cool before slicing.

SALTED BREAKFAST POTATOES

Serves: 2
Time: 15 Minutes

Ingredients:

- 1 Potatoes, Large & Diced
- 1/2 Teaspoon Oregano
- 1/4 Teaspoon Cinnamon
- 1/4 Teaspoon Smoked Paprika
- 1 Rosemary Sprig
- 1 Tablespoon Sunflower Oil
- 1 Tablespoon Butter
- Sea Salt to Taste

Directions:

1. Start by mixing your cinnamon, oregano, paprika and salt together.
2. Wash your potatoes before dicing them, and then rinsing them with cool water. Pat your potatoes dry, and then heat up your butter and oil in a skillet over medium heat. Add in your potatoes, and cook until they're done all the way through, which will take five to ten minutes.
3. Drain, and then season with the salt mixture. Mix well before serving warm.

HUEVOS REVULETOS

Serves: 2

Time: 15 Minutes

Ingredients:

- 2 Eggs
- 1 Tablespoon Butter Spread
- 1/4 Cup Tomatoes, Chopped
- 1/4 Cup Onions, Chopped
- Cilantro, Chopped Fresh to Garnish
- 3 Tablespoons Queso Fresco Cheese, Crumbled

Directions:

1. Melt the butter in a skillet using medium heat, and then once the butter is melted throw in your vegetables. Stir well, and cook for four minutes.
2. Add in the eggs, stirring often to avoid burning. Cook for an additional two minutes or until your eggs are all the way done.
3. Sprinkle with chees and cilantro before serving warm.

BANANA NUT OATMEAL

Serves: 2

Time: 5 Minutes

Ingredients:

- 2 Bananas, Peeled
- 1/2 Cup Quick Cooking Oats
- 1 Cup Skim Milk
- 6 Tablespoons Honey, Raw
- 2 Teaspoons Flaxseeds
- 4 Tablespoons Walnuts, Chopped

Directions:

1. Start by combining all ingredients except your bananas in a microwave safe bowl, and cook for two minutes on high.
2. Mash the bananas and stir it into your mixture.
3. Dish between two bowls before serving warm.

EASY MEDITERRANEAN EGGS

Serves: 2

Time: 1 Hour 10 Minutes

Ingredients:

- 3 Yellow Onions
- 4 Eggs, Large
- 1/2 Tablespoon Olive Oil
- 1/2 Tablespoon Butter
- 1 Clove Garlic, Minced
- 3 Tablespoons Tomatoes, Sun Dried
- 3 Ounces Feta Cheese
- Sea Salt & Black Pepper to Taste
- Parsley, Fresh & Chopped
- Ciabatta Rolls, Whole Grain

Directions:

1. Start by heating your oil in a skillet using medium heat, and then add in your onions. Add in your butter, and mix well.
2. Allow them to cook for about an hour. They should be brown and soft, making sure to stir every ten minutes.
3. Add in your tomatoes and garlic, and cook for three minutes more before cracking your eggs

on top. Sprinkle with salt and pepper, and then top with feta.
4. Cover with a tight lid, and cook for fifteen minutes without stirring. Serve warm.

MEDITERRANEAN OMELET

Serves: 2

Time: 10 Minutes

Ingredients:

- 1/4 Cup Red Onion, Sliced Thin
- 1/2 Yellow Bell Pepper, Sliced Thin
- 1/2 Red Bell Pepper, Sliced Thin
- 2 Teaspoons Olive Oil, Divided
- 1 Clove Garlic, Minced
- 2 Tablespoons Basil, Fresh & Chopped
- 2 Tablespoons Parsley, Fresh & Chopped + More for Garnish
- 4 Eggs, Beaten
- Sea Salt & Black Pepper

Directions:

1. Get out a heavy skillet and heat up a teaspoon of olive oil using medium heat, and then add in your bell pepper, garlic, and onion. Cook for five minutes, stirring frequently.
2. Add your basil, salt, pepper and parsley. Increase the heat o medium-high, cooking for an additional two minutes.
3. Push the vegetable mix to a plate, and then put the pan back over heat. Heat the remaining oil and pour in your eggs. Tilt until it's coated evenly at the bottom. Cook until the edges are bubbly and the center is nearly dry. This should take roughly five minutes. Flip your omelet.
4. Once your omelet has been flipped, spoon your mixture into one half, and then fold it over.
5. Cut your omelet and serve garnished with parsley.

FLANK STEAK & SPINACH SALAD

Serves: 2

Time: 30 Minutes

Ingredients:

- 1/2 lb. Flank Steak
- 1/2 Teaspoon Olive Oil
- 1 Tablespoon Garlic Powder
- Sea Salt & Black Pepper to Taste
- 2 Cups Baby Spinach

- 5 Cremini Mushrooms, Sliced
- 5 Cherry Tomatoes, Halved
- 1/4 Red Bell Pepper, Sliced Thin
- 1 Small Red Onion, Sliced Thin

Directions:

1. Get out a baking sheet and line it with foil, and then preheat your broiler.
2. Rub the steak down with olive oil, salt, pepper and garlic, allowing it to marinate for ten minutes before putting it on the pan under your broiler. Broil for five minutes, and allow it to rest for ten.
3. Get out a large bowl and combine your tomatoes, onion, mushrooms, spinach and bell pepper. Toss to combine.
4. Serve with steak sliced on top.

EASY CHICKEN GREEK SALAD

Serves: 2

Time: 15 Minutes

Ingredients:

- 1/4 Cup Balsamic Vinegar
- 1 Teaspoon Lemon Juice, Fresh
- 1/4 Cup Olive Oil
- 2 Grilled Chicken Breasts, Boneless, Skinless & Sliced
- 1/2 Cup Red Onion, Sliced Thin
- 8 Kalamata Olives, Halved & Pitted
- 10 Cherry Tomatoes, Halved
- 2 Cups Romaine Lettuce, Chopped Roughly
- 1/2 Cup Feta Cheese
- Sea Salt & Black Pepper to Taste

Directions:

1. Get out a bowl and combine your lemon juice and vinegar, stirring until it is well combined. Whisk your olive oil in slowly, and continue to whisk until well blended. Add your salt and pepper and whisk again.
2. Add in your onion, tomatoes, olives and chicken. Stir well, and then cover. Allow it to chill for at least two hours or even overnight.
3. Divide the lettuce between two plates, and top with half of your vegetables and chicken. Sprinkle your feta cheese over both plates before serving.

CHEESE STUFFED TOMATOES

Serves: 2

Time: 30 Minutes

Ingredients:

- 1/2 Cup Yellow Onion, Diced
- 1/2 lb. White Mushrooms, Sliced
- 2 Cloves Garlic, Minced
- 4 Large Tomatoes, Ripe
- 1 Tablespoon Olive Oil
- 1 Tablespoon Basil, Fresh & Chopped
- 1 Tablespoon Oregano, Fresh & Chopped
- 1 Cup Mozzarella Cheese, Shredded & Part Skim
- 1 Tablespoon Parmesan Cheese, Grated
- Sea Salt & Black Pepper to Taste

Directions:

1. Start by heating the oven to 375 before getting out a baking pan. Line it in foil, and then rinse your tomatoes. Slice a sliver from the bottom of each so they can stand on the tray, and then cut a slice from the top of each about a half an inch. Scoop the pulp out, placing it in a bowl.
2. Get a skillet out and heat up your olive using medium heat. Sauté your mushrooms, garlic, onion, basil and oregano for five minutes. Season with salt and pepper. Transfer this to a bowl, and blend with your tomato pulp. Stir in your cheese.
3. Fill each tomato loosely with the mix, topping with parmesan. Bake for fifteen to twenty minutes. Your cheese should be bubbly.

TOMATO & PASTA BOWL

Serves: 2

Time: 20 Minutes

Ingredients:

- 4 Ounces Linguine, Whole Grain
- 1 clove Garlic, Minced
- 1/2 Tablespoon Olive Oil
- 1/8 Cup Yellow Onion, Chopped
- 1/2 Teaspoon Oregano, Fresh & Chopped
- 1/2 Teaspoon Tomato Paste
- 4 Ounces Cherry Tomatoes, Halved
- 1/2 Tablespoon Parsley, Fresh & Chopped
- 1/4 Cup Parmesan Cheese, Grated
- Sea Salt & Black Pepper to Taste

Directions:

1. Get out a saucepan to boil water over high heat, cooking the linguine according the package. Drain, and reserve a half a cup of the pasta water, but do not rinse your pasta.
2. Get out a heavy skillet and place it over medium-high heat to heat up your olive oi. Sauté your oregano, garlic and onion for five minutes.
3. Add in the tomato paste, ¼ cup of pasta water, and season with salt and pepper. Cook for a minute.
4. Stir in your tomatoes next as well as your cooked pasta, adding more pasta water if needed.
5. Top with parmesan and parsley before serving.

GARLIC BROILED SARDINES

Serves: 2

Time: 15 Minutes

Ingredients:

- 2 Cloves Garlic, Minced
- 1 Tablespoon Olive Oil (Only if your Sardines are packed in water)
- 1/4 Teaspoon Red Pepper Flakes
- Sea Salt & Black Pepper to Taste
- 2 Cans Sardines (3.25 Ounces Each)

Directions:

1. Start by preheating your broiler before getting out a baking dish. Line the baking dish with foil before arranging your sardines on the bottom in a single layer.
2. Combine your olive oil, red pepper flakes and garlic in a bowl, spooning it over the sardines.
3. Sprinkle sea salt and black pepper over them, and then broiler for three minutes. Serve warm.

FRUITY CHICKEN SALAD

Serves: 2

Time: 15 Minutes

Ingredients:

- 1/4 Cup Celery, Diced
- 1/4 Cup Red Onion, Diced
- 1/2 Cup Cranberries, Dried
- 2 Cups Chicken Breast, Cooked & Chopped
- 2 Granny Smith Apples, Peeled, Cored & Diced
- 2 Tablespoons Honey Dijon Mustard
- 1 Tablespoons Olive Oil Based Mayonnaise
- Sea Salt & Black Pepper to Taste

Directions:

1. Get outa bowl and combine your cranberries, chicken, apples, celery and onion. Mix until well combined.
2. Get out another bowl and mix your mayonnaise, salt, pepper and mustard. Whisk well until it's blended. Stir your dressing into the chicken mixture, making sure it's well combined before serving.

MUSTARD TROUT WITH APPLES

Serves: 2

Time: 1 Hour 5 Minutes

Ingredients;

- 1 Tablespoon Olive Oil
- 1 Small Shallot, Minced
- 2 Lady Apples, Halved
- 4 Trout Fillets, 3 Ounces Each
- 1 1/2 Tablespoons Bread Crumbs, Plain & Fine
- 1/2 Teaspoon Thyme, Fresh & Chopped
- 1/2 Tablespoon Butter, Melted & Unsalted
- 1/2 Cup Apple Cider
- 1 Teaspoon Light Brown Sugar
- 1/2 Tablespoon Dijon Mustard
- 1/2 Tablespoon Capers, Rinsed
- Sea Salt & Black Pepper to Taste

Directions:

1. Start by heating your oven to 375, and then get out a small bowl. Combine your bread crumbs, shallot and thyme before seasoning with salt and pepper.
2. Add in the butter, and mix well.
3. Put the apples cut side up in a baking dish, and then sprinkle with sugar. Top with bread crumbs, and then pour half of your cider around the apples, covering the dish. Bake for a half an hour.
4. Uncover, and then bake for twenty more minutes. The apples should be tender but your crumbs should be crisp. Remove the apples from the oven.
5. Turn the broiler on, and then put the rack four inches away. Pat your trout down, and then season with salt and pepper. Brush your oil on a baking sheet, and then put your trout with the skin side up. Brush your remaining oil over the skin, and broil for six minutes. It should be cooked all the way through. Repeat the apples on the shelf right below the trout. This will keep the crumbs from burning, and it should only take two minutes to heat up.
6. Get out a saucepan, and whisk your remaining cider, capers, and mustard together. Add more cider if necessary to thin, and cook for five minutes on medium-high. It should have a sauce

- 1/4 Cup Green Olives, Pitted & Chopped
- 3 Tablespoons Raisins
- 1/3 Cup Chickpeas, Canned, Drained & Rinsed
- 2 Sprigs Thyme, Fresh

Directions:

1. Start by heating your oven to 350, and then get out a Dutch oven or oven safe skillet. Heat your olive oil using medium heat, and then place the chicken in the skillet. Make sure that the pan isn't overcrowded. Sauté for five minutes per side, which should make your chicken crisp. Transfer it to a plate, and place the chicken to the side for now.
2. Reduce the heat to medium-low, throwing in your garlic, ginger, onion and carrots. Sauté, and make sure to stir frequently as to not burn your onion. Your onion should soften in five minutes, and then throw in your wine, broth and water. Bring it to a boil to deglaze the pan.
3. Add your chicken back in, and then add in your thyme. Bring it up to a boil again, and then place it in the oven. Cook for forty-five minutes.
4. Take it out of the oven, and stir in your olives, raisins, and chickpeas. Return it to the oven, braising while uncovered for twenty minutes. Discard the thyme before serving.

LAMB & COUSCOUS SALAD

Serves: 2

Time: 25 Minutes

Ingredients:

- 1/2 Cup Water
- 1/2 Tablespoon Garlic, Minced
- 1 1/4 lb. Lamb Loin Chops, Trimmed
- 1/4 Cup Couscous, Whole Wheat
- Pinch Sea Salt
- 1/2 Tablespoon Parsley, Fresh & Chopped Fine
- 1 Tomato, Chopped
- 1 Teaspoon Olive Oil
- 1 Small Cucumber, Peeled & Chopped
- 1 1/2 Tablespoons Lemon Juice, Fresh
- 1/4 Cup Feta, Crumbled
- 1 Tablespoon Dill, Fresh & Chopped Fine

Directions:

1. Get out a saucepan and bring the water to a boil.
2. Get out a bowl and mix your garlic, salt and parsley. Press this mixture into the side of each lamb chop, and then heat your oil using medium-high heat in a skillet.
3. Add the lamb, cooking for six minutes per side. Place it to the side, and cover to help keep the lamb chops warm.
4. Stir the couscous into the water once it's started to boil, returning it to a boil before reducing

it to low so that it simmers. Cover, and then cook for about two minutes more. Remove from heat, and allow it to stand uncovered for five minutes. Fluff using a fork, and then add in your tomatoes, lemon juice, feta and dill. Stir well. Serve on the side of your lamb chops.

Serves: 2

Time: 45 Minutes

Ingredients:

- 1/2 lb. Shrimp with Shells
- 1 Small Onion, Chopped
- 1/2 Cup White Wine
- 1 Tablespoon Parsley, Fresh & Chopped
- 8 Ounces Tomatoes, Canned & Diced
- 3 Tablespoons Olive Oil
- 4 Ounces Feta Cheese
- Cubed Salt
- Dash Black Pepper
- 14 Teaspoon Garlic Powder

Directions:

1. Get out a saucepan and then pour in about two inches of water, bringing it to a boil. Boil for five minutes, and then drain but reserve the liquid. Set both the shrimp and the liquid to the side.
2. Heat two tablespoons of oil up next, and when heated add in your onions. Cook until the onions are translucent. Mix in your parsley, garlic, wine, olive oil and tomatoes. Simmer for a half hour, and stir until it's thickened.
3. Remove the legs of the shrimp, pulling off the shells, head and tail.
4. Add the shrimp and shrimp stock into the sauce once it's thickened. Bring it to a simmer for five minutes, and then add the feta cheese.
5. Let it stand until the cheese starts to melt, and then serve warm.

MEDITERRANEAN SALMON

Serves: 2

Time: 30 Minutes

Ingredients:

- 2 Salmon Fillets, Skinless & 6 Ounces Each1
- 1 Cup Cherry Tomatoes
- 1 Tablespoon Capers
- 1/4 Cup Zucchini, Chopped Fine
- 1/8 Teaspoon Black Pepper
- 1/8 Teaspoon Sea Salt, Fine

- 1/2 Tablespoon Olive Oil
- 1.25 Ounces Ripe Olives, Sliced

Directions:

1. Start by heating your oven to 425, and then sprinkle your salt and pepper over your fish on both sides. Place the fish in a single layer on your baking dish after coating your baking dish using cooking spray.
2. Combine the tomatoes and remaining ingredients, spooning the mixture over your fillets, and then bake for twenty-two minutes. Serve warm.

SEAFOOD LINGUINE

Serves: 2

Time: 45 Minutes

Ingredients:

- 2 Cloves Garlic, Chopped
- 4 Ounces Linguine, Whole Wheat
- 1 Tablespoon Olive Oil
- 14 Ounces Tomatoes, Canned & Diced
- 1/2 Tablespoon Shallot, Chopped
- 1/4 Cup White Wine
- Sea Salt & Black Pepper to Taste
- 6 Cherrystone Clams, Cleaned
- 4 Ounces Tilapia, Sliced into 1 Inch Strips
- 4 Ounces Dry Sea Scallops
- 1/8 Cup Parmesan Cheese, Grated
- 1/2 Teaspoon Marjoram, Chopped & Fresh

Directions:

1. Get a pot of water and bring it to a boil, cooking your pasta until tender which should take roughly eight minutes. Drain and then rinse your pasta.
2. Heat your oil using a large skillet over medium heat, and then once your oil is hot add in your garlic and shallot. Cook for a minute, and stir often.
3. Increase the heat to medium-high before adding your salt, wine, pepper and tomatoes, bringing it to a simmer. Cook for one minute more.
4. Add your clams next, covering and cooking for another two minutes.
5. Stir in your marjoram, scallops and fish next. Cover, and cook until the fish is done all the way through and your clams have opened up.t his will take up to five minutes, and get rid of any clams that do not open.
6. Spoon the sauce and your clams over the pasta, sprinkling with parmesan and marjoram before serving. Serve warm.

GINGER SHRIMP & TOMATO RELISH

Serves: 2

Time: 25 Minutes

Ingredients:

- 1 1/2 Tablespoons Vegetable Oil
- 1 Clove Garlic, Minced
- 10 Shrimp, Extra Large, Peeled & Tails Left On
- 3/4 Tablespoons Finger, Grated & Peeled
- 1 Green Tomatoes, Halved
- 2 Plum Tomatoes, Halved
- 1 Tablespoon Lime Juice, Fresh
- 1/2 Teaspoon Sugar
- 1/2 Tablespoon Jalapeno with Seeds, Fresh & Minced
- 1/2 Tablespoon Basil, Fresh & Chopped
- 1/2 Tablespoons Cilantro, Chopped & Fresh
- 10 Skewers
- Sea Salt & Black Pepper to Taste

Directions:

1. Soak your skewers in a pan of water for at least a half hour.
2. Stir your garlic and ginger together in a bowl, transferring half to a larger bowl and stirring it with two tablespoons of your oil. Add in the shrimp, and make sure they are well coated.
3. Cover and place it in the fridge for at least a half hour, and then allow it to refrigerate.
4. Heat your grill to high, and grease the grates lightly using oil. Get out a bowl and toss your plum and green tomatoes with the remaining tablespoon of oil, seasoning with salt and pepper.
5. Grill your tomatoes with the cut side up and the skins should be charred. The flesh of your tomato should be tender, which will take about four to six minutes for the plum tomato and about ten minutes for the green tomato.
6. Remove the skins once the tomatoes are cool enough to handle, and then discard the seeds. Chop the tomatoes flesh fine, adding it to the reserved ginger and garlic. Add in your sugar, jalapeno, lime juice and basil.
7. Season your shrimp using salt and pepper threading them onto the skewers, and then grill until they turn opaque, which is about two minutes on each side. Place the shrimp on a platter with your relish and enjoy.

SHRIMP & PASTA

Serves: 2

Time: 20 Minutes

Ingredients:

- 2 Cups Angel Hair Pasta, Cooked
- 1/2 lb. Medium Shrimp, Peeled
- 1 Clove Garlic, Minced
- 1 Cup Tomato, Chopped
- 1 Teaspoon Olive Oil
- 1/6 Cup Kalamata Olives, Pitted & Chopped
- 1/8 Cup Basil, Fresh & Sliced Thin
- 1 Tablespoon Capers, Drained
- 1/8 Cup Feta Cheese, Crumbled
- Dash Black Pepper

Directions:

1. Cook your pasta per package instructions, and then heat up your olive oil in a skillet using medium-high heat. Cook your garlic for half a minute, and then add your shrimp. Sauté for a minute more.
2. Add your basil and tomato, and then reduce the heat to allow it to simmer for three minutes. Your tomato should be tender.
3. Stir in your olives and capers. Add a dash of black pepper, and combine your shrimp mix and pasta together to serve. Top with cheese before serving warm.

POACHED COD

Serves: 2

Time: 35 Minutes

Ingredients:

- 2 Cod Filets, 6 Ounces
- Sea Salt & Black Pepper to Taste
- 1/4 Cup Dry White Wine
- 1/4 Cup Seafood Stock
- 2 Cloves Garlic, Minced
- 1 Bay Leaf
- 1/2 Teaspoon Sage, Fresh & Chopped
- 2 Rosemary Sprigs to Garnish

Directions:

1. Start by turning your oven to 375, and then season the fillets with salt and pepper. Place them in a baking pan, and add in your stock, garlic, wine, sage and bay leaf. Cover well, and then bake for twenty minutes. Your fish should be flaky when tested with a fork.
2. Use a spatula to remove each fillet, placing the liquid over high heat and cooking to reduce in half. This should take ten minutes, and you need to stir frequently.
3. Serve dripped in poaching liquid and garnished with a rosemary sprig.

MUSSELS IN WHITE WINE

Serves: 2

Time: 15 Minutes

Ingredients:

- 2 lbs. Live Mussels, Fresh
- 1 Cup Dry White Wine
- 1/4 Teaspoon Sea Salt, Fine
- 3 Cloves Garlic, Minced
- 2 Teaspoons Shallots, Diced
- 1/4 Cup Parsley, Fresh & Chopped, Divided
- 2 Tablespoons olive Oil
- 1/4 Lemon, Juiced

Directions:

1. Get out a colander and scrub your mussels, rinsing them using cold water. Discard mussels that will not close if they're tapped, and then use a paring knife to remove the beard from each one.
2. Get out stockpot, placing it over medium-high heat, and add in your garlic, shallots, wine and parsley. Bring it to a simmer. Once it's at a steady simmer, add in your mussels and cover. Allow them to simmer for five to seven minutes. Make sure they do not overcook.
3. Use a slotted spoon to remove them, and add your lemon juice and olive oil into the pot. Stir well, and pour the broth over your mussels before serving with parsley.

DILLY SALMON

Serves: 2

Time: 25 Minutes

Ingredients:

- 2 Salmon Fillets, 6 Ounces Each
- 1 Tablespoon Olive Oil
- 1/2 Tangerine, Juiced
- 2 Teaspoons Orange Zest
- 2 Tablespoons Dill, Fresh & Chopped
- Sea Salt & Black Pepper to Taste

Directions:

1. Start by heating your oven to 375, and then get out two ten-inch pieces of foil. Rub your filets down with olive oil on both side before seasoning with salt and pepper, placing each fillet into a piece of foil.
2. Drizzle your orange juice over each one, and then top with orange zest and dill. Fold your

packet closed, making sure it has two inches of air space within the foil so your fish can steam, and then place them on a baking dish.
3. Bake for fifteen minutes before opening the packets, and transfer to two serving plates. Pour the sauce over the top of each before serving.

CHICKEN & VEGETABLE SOUP

Serves: 2

Time: 30 Minutes

Ingredients:

- 1/2 Cup Parsley, Fresh & Chopped + More for Garnish
- 1 Teaspoon Olive Oil
- 1 Yellow Onion, Diced
- 1 Carrot, Large, Peeled & Diced
- 1 Celery Stalk, Peeled & diced
- 2 Chicken Breasts, Boneless, Skinless, 6 Ounces Each & Cut into 1-inch Pieces
- 1 Zucchini, Diced
- 2 Yellow Squash, Diced
- 1 Teaspoon Basil, Fresh & Chopped
- 2 Cups Chicken Stock
- Sea Salt & Black Pepper to Taste

Directions:

1. Get out a heavy skillet and heat your olive oil over medium-high heat. Add in your celery, onion and carrot. Sauté for five minutes, making sure to sit frequently. Add in your chicken, cooking for another ten minutes while stirring often.
2. Add in your squash and zucchini before mixing in your basil, parsley and oregano. Season with salt and pepper, and cook for five minutes. Reduce the heat, and pour in the stock. Cover, cooking for another ten minutes.
3. Ladle into bowl and serve garnished with parsley.

SIDE DISHES & SNACKS

SAUTÉED SPINACH & PINE NUTS

Serves: 2

Time: 10 Minutes

Ingredients:

- 10 Ounce Bag Spinach, Fresh

- 2 Tablespoons Golden Raisins
- 2 Cloves Garlic, Minced
- 2 Teaspoons Olive Oil
- 1 Tablespoon Parmesan Cheese, Shaved
- 1 Tablespoon Pine Nuts
- 2 Teaspoons Balsamic Vinegar
- Sea Salt & Black Pepper to Taste

Directions:

1. Heat the oil in a skillet using medium-high heat, and then cook your garlic, raisin and pine nuts for a half a minute. Stir well to keep from burning, and then add in your spinach. Cover your pan and allow it to wilt for two minutes.
2. Remove from heat, and then add in your vinegar and salt.
3. Top with cheese and pepper before serving.

FRENCH ONION SOUP

Serves: 2

Time: 30 Minutes

Ingredients:

- 8 Ounces Chickpeas, Rinsed
- 14 Ounces Beef Broth, Reduced Sodium
- 1 Tablespoon Olive Oil
- 1 Small Sweet Onion, Sliced
- 1 Tablespoon Sherry
- 1 Leek, Chopped
- 1/2 Teaspoon Thyme, Fresh & Chopped
- 2 Tablespoons Garlic, Chopped
- 2 Slices Whole Wheat Bread, Toasted
- 2 Tablespoons Chives, Fresh & Minced
- 1/3 Cup Gruyere, Shredded
- Black Pepper to Taste

Directions:

1. Heat your oil in a skillet using medium-high heat. Add in your onion, and then reduce to medium to cook stir often until it's softened and brown. This will take up to eight minutes.
2. Throw in your garlic, thyme and leek, cooking for four minutes more. Stir often.
3. Add in the pepper and sherry, and then increase it to medium-high heat again. Stir well and cook until almost all of the liquid has evaporated. This will take less than a minute, and then stir in your broth and chickpeas. Bring it to a boil, and reduce the heat to allow it to simmer. Cook until the vegetables are tender, which will take three minutes. Remove from heat before stirring in the chives.

4. Place your bread at the bottom of two bowls, topping with cheese and ladling your soup over each one.

BRAISED KALE & TOMATOES

Serves: 2

Time: 20 Minutes

Ingredients:

- 1/2 lb. Kale, Chopped
- 2 Cloves Garlic, Sliced Thin
- 1 Teaspoon Olive Oil
- 1/2 Cup Cherry Tomatoes, Halved
- 1/4 Cup Vegetable Stock
- 1/2 Tablespoon Lemon Juice, Fresh
- Sea Salt & Black Pepper to Taste

Directions:

1. Heat your olive oil in a frying pan using medium heat, and then sauté your garlic for two minutes.
2. Add in your vegetable stock and kale, and then cover. Reduce the heat to medium-low, and allow it to wilt. It will take five minutes.
3. Stir in your tomatoes, and cook uncovered for seven minutes. Remove from heat, and season with salt, pepper and lemon juice before serving warm.

ANCHOVY & OLIVE SALAD

Serves: 2

Time: 40 Minutes

Ingredients:

- 3 Anchovy Fillets
- 1/2 Small Red Onion, Sliced Thin
- 8 Black Olives, Salt Cured, Pitted & Halved
- 2 Small Blood Oranges
- 1 1/2 Tablespoons Olive Oil
- 1/2 Tablespoon Lemon Juice, Fresh
- 1 Teaspoon Fennel Fronts, Minced Fine
- 1/2 Tablespoon Lemon Juice, Fresh
- 1/8 Teaspoon Black Pepper

Directions:

1. Peel the orange carefully and cut away the membrane and pith. Make sure to capture all the juices, and slice the oranges into rounds.
2. Arrange them on a platter, and reserve the juice in a bowl. Distribute your onions over the oranges, and then top with olive and anchovy fillets. Drizzle with oil, and let it marinate for a half hour before serving sprinkled with fennel fronts.

GREEK POTATOES

Serves: 2

Time: 2 Hours 30 Minutes

Ingredients:

- 1 Cube Chicken Bouillon
- 3 Pantoates, Peeled & Quartered
- 1/6 Cup Olive Oil
- 1 Clove Garlic, Chopped Fine
- 3/4 Cup Water
- 1/8 Cup Lemon Juice, Fresh
- 1/2 Teaspoon Thyme
- 1/2 Teaspoon Rosemary
- Sea Salt & Black Pepper to Taste

Directions:

1. Start by heating your oven to 350.
2. Mix your olive oil, thyme, garlic, rosemary, pepper, lemon juice, bouillon and water in a bowl.
3. Arrange the potatoes in a baking dish, pouring the mixture over them, and bake for one and a half to two hours. Turn occasionally to keep from burning, and serve warm.

SPICY EGGPLANT

Serves: 2

Time: 50 Minutes

Ingredients:

- 1 Shallot, Sliced
- 1 Small Eggplant
- 1 1/2 Tablespoons Sherry Wine Vinegar
- 1 Clove Garlic, Minced
- 1/2 Tablespoon Sugar
- 1 Tablespoon Golden Raisins

- Dash Red Pepper Flakes
- 1/2 Tablespoon Capers
- 1/8 Cup + 2 Teaspoons Olive Oil
- 2 Gaeta Olives, Pitted & Chopped
- Vegetable Oil
- Sea Salt to Taste

Directions:

1. Slice the eggplant crosswise, slicing it into eight slices. Sprinkle with salt, and then place the pieces in a colander. Allow them to drain for a half hour, and then rinse the eggplant off before patting it dry.
2. Get out a sauce pan and place it over medium heat. Add your red pepper flakes, vinegar, sugar, garlic, shallots, sugar and two tablespoons of water. Bring it to a boil, cooking for a minute before taking it off of heat. Stir in your capers, olives, raisins, and 1/8 cup olive oil. Mix well and allow it to cool to room temperature.
3. Heat the grill to high, and make sure to oil the grates using vegetable oil. Brush the eggplant with two teaspoons of olive oil. Cook the eggplant until charred and tender. Turn it halfway through.
4. Arrange it on a platter, spooning the shallot mixture on top to serve.

SPICED TURKEY & GRAPEFRUIT RELISH

Serves: 2

Time: 15 Minutes

Ingredients:

Relish:

- 1 Grapefruit, Seedless
- 1 Small Shallot, Minced
- 1 Teaspoon Red Wine Vinegar
- 1 Teaspoon Honey, Raw
- 1/2 Small Avocado, Pitted, Peeled & Diced
- 1 Tablespoon Cilantro, Fresh & Chopped

Spiced Turkey:

- 2 Turkey Cutlets, 8 Ounces Each
- 1/2 Teaspoon Five Spice Powder
- 1 Tablespoon Chili Powder
- 1 Tablespoon Olive Oil
- Pinch Sea Salt, Fine

Directions:

1. Start by peeling your grapefruit and cutting away the white pith. Cut the fruit into segments, making sure to remove the membrane. Squeeze any juice that remains in a bowl, and then add in your vinegar, shallots, honey, avocado and cilantro. Toss to combine, and then set it to the side.
2. Combine the chili powder, salt and five spice powder, coating your turkey in the mixture.
3. Heat the oil in a skillet over medium-high heat, cooking your turkey for three minutes per side. It should still be pink in the middle when you remove it from the pan.
4. Divide your turkey between plates, adding your relish on the side to serve.

GREEK CHICKEN PENNE

Serves: 2

Time: 20 Minutes

Ingredients:

- 1 Clove Garlic, Minced
- 8 Ounces Penne Pasta
- 1/2 lb. Chicken Breast Halves, Boneless, Skinless & Chopped
- 1/4 Cup Red Onion, Chopped
- 3/4 Tablespoon Butter
- 8 Ounces Artichoke Hearts, Canned
- 1 Small Tomato, Chopped
- 1 1/2 Tablespoons Parsley, Fresh & Chopped
- 1/4 Cup Feta Cheese, Crumbled
- 1 Tablespoon Lemon Juice, Fresh
- 1/2 Teaspoon Oregano
- Sea Salt & Black Pepper to Taste

Directions:

1. Start by cooking your pasta per package instructions so that it's al dente. Drain your pasta and place it to the side.
2. Get out a skillet and melt your butter over medium-high heat. Cook your onion and garlic for two minutes before adding in your chicken. Cook for six more minutes, making sure to stir occasionally to keep it from burning.
3. Reduce the heat to medium-low before draining and chopping your artichoke hearts. Throw them in the skillet with your parsley, tomato, oregano, lemon juice, feta cheese and drained pasta. Heat all the ay through and cook for three minutes.
4. Season with salt and pepper, and serve warm.

LEMON CAPER CHICKEN

Serves: 2

Time: 20 Minutes

Ingredients:

- 1/4 Teaspoon Black Pepper
- 1/2 Cup Dry Bread Crumbs
- 1 Egg
- 3/4 lb. Chicken Breast Halves, Skinless & Boneless (Pounded 3/4 Inch Thick & Sliced)
- 3 Tablespoons Capers
- 1 Lemon, Cut into Wedges

Directions:

1. Start by beating your eggs with your pepper, mixing in the bread crumbs.
2. Get out a skillet and heat your olive oil using medium heat. Dip the chicken into the egg mixture, spreading the bread crumbs into the chicken, shaking any lose ones off. Fry the chicken in the pan for about eight minutes per side so that it becomes golden brown.
3. Drizzle your chicken with caper juice, and serve with lemon wedges.

GNOCCHI WITH SHRIMP

Serves: 4

Time: 20 Minutes

Ingredients:

- 1/2 lb. Shrimp, Peeled & Deveined
- 1/4 Cup Shallots, Sliced
- 1/2 Tablespoon + 1 Teaspoon Olive Oil
- 8 Ounces Shelf Stable Gnocchi
- 1/2 Bunch Asparagus, Cut into Thirds
- 3 Tablespoons Parmesan Cheese
- 1 Tablespoon Lemon Juice, Fresh
- 1/3 Cup Chicken Broth
- Sea Salt & Black Pepper to Taste

Directions:

1. Start by heating a half a tablespoon of oil over medium heat, and then add in your gnocchi. Cook while stirring often until they turn plump and golden. This will take from seven to ten minutes. Place them in a bowl.
2. Heat your remaining teaspoon of oil with your shallots, cooking until they begin to brown. Make sure to stir, but this will take two minutes. Stir in the broth before adding your asparagus. Cover, and cook for three to four minutes.
3. Add the shrimp, seasoning with salt and pepper. Cook until they are pink and cooked through, which will take roughly four minutes.
4. Return the gnocchi to the skillet with lemon juice, cooking for another two minutes. Stir well, and then remove it from heat.

5. Sprinkle with parmesan, and let it stand for two minutes. Your cheese should melt. Serve warm.

MEDITERRANEAN FRIED RICE

Serves: 2

Time: 15 Minutes

Ingredients:

- 3/4 Cup Rice, Cooked
- 1 Clove Garlic, Minced
- 1 Tablespoon Olive Oil
- 5 Ounces Chopped Spinach, Thawed & Drained
- 1/4 Cup Feta Cheese with Herbs, Crumbled
- 2 Ounces Roasted Red Pepper, Drained & Chopped
- 3 Ounce Marinated Artichoke Hearts, Drained & Quartered

Directions:

1. Start by heating your olive oil over medium heat in a skillet and then add in your garlic. Cook for two minutes, and then add in your rice. Cook for an additional two minutes and make sure to stir frequently to keep it from burning.
2. Add in the spinach, cooking for an additional three minutes, and then stir in your roasted red peppers. Add the artichoke hearts, cooking for an additional two minutes.
3. Throw in the feta and mix before removing from heat. Serve warm.

SWISS CHARD & OLIVES

Serves: 2

Time: 15 Minutes

Ingredients:

- 3/4 lb. Swiss Chard
- 1/2 Yellow Onion, Sliced
- 1/2 Jalapeno Pepper, Chopped Fine
- 1/6 Cup Kalamata Olives, Pitted & Chopped
- 1/2 Teaspoon Olive Oil
- 1/4 Cup Water

Directions:

1. Remove he stem of your Swiss chard from your leaves, and chop the leaves. Set them to the side and cut the stem into one-inch pieces.
2. Get out a skillet and place your oil over medium heat, adding in your onion, garlic and

jalapeno. Cook until your onion becomes translucent. This will take roughly six minutes.
3. Add in your olives, water and swiss chard. Cover the skillet, cooking for three minutes more. Stir until the swiss chard leaves and steam are tender, which takes about five more minutes.

CUCUMBER & PESTO BOATS

Serves: 2

Time: 20 Minutes

Ingredients:

- 2 Small Cucumbers
- 1/4 Teaspoon Sea Salt, Fine
- 1/2 Cup Basil, Fresh & Packed
- 1 Clove Garlic, Minced
- 1/8 Cup Walnut Pieces
- 1/8 Cup Parmesan Cheese, Grated
- 1/8 Cup Olive Oil
- 1/4 Teaspoon Paprika

Directions:

1. Cut your cucumbers in half lengthwise, and again crosswise to make four pieces each. Use a spoon to hollow the seeds out and create a shell. Salt each piece, putting it to the side.
2. Get out a blender and combine your garlic, basil, walnuts, olive oil and parmesan. Blend until it makes a smooth mixture, and then spread it over your "boats". Sprinkle with paprika before serving.

CITRUS MELON

Serves: 2

Time: 4 Hours 10 Minutes

Ingredients:

- 1 Cups Melon, Cubed (Sharlyn, Crenshaw or Honeydew)
- 1 Cup Cantaloupe, Cubed
- 1/4 Cup Orange Juice, Fresh
- 1/8 Cup Lime Juice, Fresh
- 1/2 Tablespoon Orange Zest

Directions:

1. Combine both melons in a bowl, and then get out a small bow whisk your orange zest, lime juice and orange juice together. Pour it over your fruit, and mix well.
2. Cover and allow it to set in the fridge for four hours. You'll need to stir occasionally. Serve

cold.

YOGURT MOUSSE & SOUR CHERRY TOPPING

Serves: 2

Time: 4 Hours 20 Minutes

Ingredients:

- 1/2 Cup Heavy Cream, Well Chilled
- 3 Ounces Yogurt, Plain & Unsweetened
- 1/4 Teaspoon Vanilla Extract, Pure
- 1 Tablespoon Gelatin, Unflavored
- 3 Tablespoons Sugar
- 1 Cup Sour Cherry, Pureed Slightly

Directions:

1. Get out a small saucepan, and then sprinkle in your gelatin over ¼ cup of cold water, allowing it to soften for a minute. Heat your mixture using low heat, and stir until all of the gelatin powder has dissolved.
2. Blend your sugar, vanilla and sour cherry puree into the gelatin mix, making sure it's mixed well.
3. Transfer it to a bowl, and then stir the yogurt in.
4. Beat the cream until stiff peaks form. Fold in the cherry mixture, and then let it set in the fridge for four hours. Garnish with drained cherry preserves before serving chilled.

CARAMEL ROASTED FIGS

Serves: 2

Time: 45 Minutes

Ingredients:

- 1/4 Cup Sugar
- Whipped Cream
- 6 Figs, Ripe but Slightly Firm

Directions:

1. Start by heating the oven to 450, and then get out a baking dish. Rinse your figs and then arrange them on the baking dish standing up.
2. Get out a skillet and then pour in your sugar, making sure it's spread evenly over the bottom. Put it over medium-low heat.

3. The sugar should start to melt around the edges, and then shake the pan, and continue to let it melt. The sugar will turn a deep honey color, and then start tilting, swirling and shaking to distribute the sugar evenly. Don't poke at it, and make sure to be patient.
4. All of your sugar should be completely melted and turning an amber color. This will take about fifteen minutes.
5. Pour this over your figs, and then roast until big bubbles form and the caramel turns a deep amber. This should take about fifteen minutes more. Serve garnished with whipped cream.

POMEGRANATE POACHED PEARS

Serves: 2

Time: 1 Hour 10 Minutes

Ingredients:

- 1/4 Cup Pomegranate Seeds
- 3/4 Cup Pomegranate Juice
- 1/2 Cup Sweet Dessert Wine
- 2 Bosc Pears, Ripe & Firm

Directions:

1. Pele your pears, and then leave them whole. The steam should be intact, and then slice off the bases so that they stand upright, and then use a cover to remove the cores, working form the base up.
2. Put your pears on the sides in a saucepan, and pour in your pomegranate juice and wine. Bring it to a simmer using medium-high heat, and then cover. Reduce the heat to low, simmering until the pears turn tender. This will take thirty to forty-five minutes, and you should turn them once or even twice to make sure that they color evenly.
3. Remove them from the skillet using a slotted spoon, and then place them in a shallow bowl.
4. Boil the liquid over high heat until it thickens and is reduced to roughly a half a cup, which will take up to twenty minutes.
5. Spoon a tablespoon of this sauce over each pear, and then sprinkle with pomegranate seeds before serving.

MARINATED BERRIES

Serves: 2

Time: 20 Minutes

Ingredients:

- 2 Shortbread Biscuits
- 1/2 Cup Blueberries, Fresh

- 1/2 Cup Raspberries, Fresh
- 1/2 Cup Strawberries, Sliced
- 1 Teaspoon Vanilla Extract, Pure
- 2 Tablespoons Brown Sugar
- 1/4 Cup Balsamic Vinegar

Directions:

1. Get out a bowl and whisk your vanilla, brown sugar and balsamic vinegar together.
2. In a different bowl add your raspberries, blueberries and strawberries together, pouring the vinegar mixture over it.
3. Allow it to marinate for fifteen minutes, and then serve over shortbread.